What Really Matters Now...

BY SUSAN & TODD MONTGOMERY

 PETER PAUPER PRESS, INC.
White Plains, New York

To our children, Liz, Kristin, Tripp, and David,
who inspired us to create this book

Photography Portfolio: www.toddmontgomery.com

Photo credits appear on pages 82-83.

Copyright © 2003
Peter Pauper Press, Inc.
202 Mamaroneck Avenue
White Plains, NY 10601
All rights reserved
ISBN 978-0-88088-192-0
Printed in China

7   6   5

Visit us at www.peterpauper.com

What Really
Matters Now...

Preface

The terror of September 11 and the ongoing war our country is waging on terrorism have made us all step back and take a look at our lives. We're asking ourselves: "What really matters now?"

We're also learning what really doesn't matter.

Our three adult children live and work and raise their families in New York City. Like all Americans, they suffered loss on September 11. Not only did they lose people they knew and worked with, they lost the uninhibited sense of joy and security they had found in their wonderful adopted city . . . and in their lives. They also lost their confidence in the future, at least temporarily. Our children's experience reflects the experience of countless people, young and old, across our country, and across the world.

While those of us who are older have had more experience with loss, we know it is never easy to deal with the disappearance of a loved one or the erosion of our faith in the future. We also know we have to pick up the pieces and go on. We have learned as we go through life—losing parents, losing leaders, losing dreams—that what sustains us are the things that are not lost—the everyday pleasures in life, the small miracles and blessings. We need to focus on these good things to help us get through tough times.

That is the resounding message in this little book: Savor life because life is fragile and life is precious—an uncomplicated and even obvious piece of advice but one which, in this time of uncertainty, is sometimes hard to embrace.

So this book is for all the children and parents and grandparents and well-meaning people everywhere who have had to learn too much too fast.

Our message is this:

Focus your lives on what really matters and you'll be OK.

Susan and Todd Montgomery

What really matters is...

always dreaming

of the mountains

yet to climb.

What really matters is

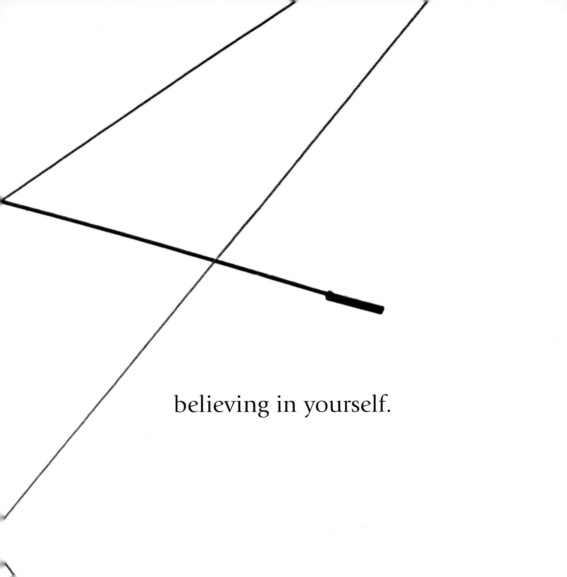

believing in yourself.

What really matters is…

letting it
all **out**.

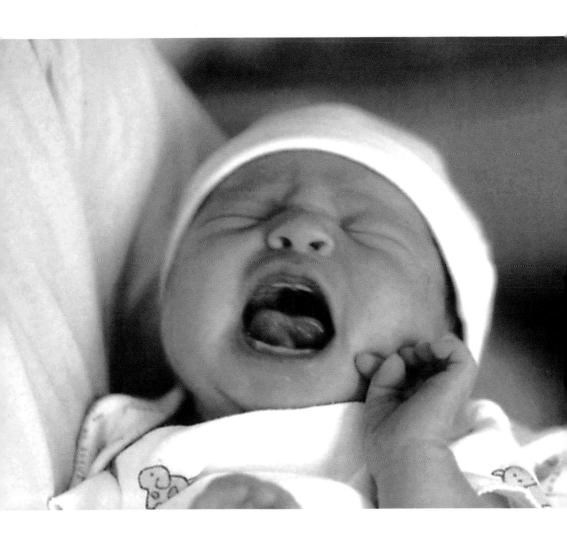

What really
matters is...

*pursuing
joy every day.*

What really matters
is embracing the

solitude.

What really matters is . . .

growing old
with a smile.

What really matters is...

*having
a friend
you can
trust.*

What really matters is

dancing through life.

What

really

matters is

enjoying

the

moment.

WHAT REALLY MATTERS IS

FINDING A QUIET PLACE TO READ.

making your own music.

What really matters is

doing your job well.

What really matters is

*a brand new
baby to love.*

What really matters is

playing the game with all your heart.

What really matters is

being together.

What really matters is

having fun by yourself.

What really matters is

sharing
the fun.

What really
matters
is
being
with
your
friends.

What really matters is

celebrating together.

What really matters is

catching the WAVE.

What really matters is

savoring your accomplishments.

What really matters is

*staying
in
awe.*

What really
matters
is learning
to share.

What really matters is
being *silly* sometimes.

What really matters is carrying on traditions.

WHAT REALLY MATTERS IS

holding hands.

*What really matters
is discovering*

YOU CAN
DO IT!

What really
matters is . . .

exploring your artistic self.

What really matters is

**simply . . .
a good loaf of bread.**

What really matters is

letting your spirit soar.

What really matters is

capturing the
rhythm of life.

What
really
matters is
staying
connected.

What really matters is

**feeling
the spirit.**

What really matters is

having the courage to take the next step.

What really matters is calling to say I love you.

What really matters is

*following
the sun.*

What really matters
is having faith

. . . in people
. . . in yourself
. . . in God.

What really matters now is

*holding on
to the memories*

*. . . and focusing on
the future.*

Photo Credits

All photos were taken by Todd Montgomery except where indicated.

Cover Photo:
Holding Hands
© Marks Productions/The Image Bank

Makalu, Nepal, 1974 7

The Great Wallenda,
Milwaukee, 1973 8-9

Libby, Day 3,
New York City, August, 2001 11

Joy in Central Park,
New York City, 1999 12-13

Alone on Black's Beach,
La Jolla, California, 1998 14-15

Sherpa, Nepal, 1974....................17

Waiting Patiently,
Manhattan, 1999 18-19

Win and Schomer at His 90th,
Milwaukee, 1996 20-21

Dueling Rafts,
Bordighera, Italy, 2001
(Photographer: Alexander
Henry)....................................22-23

What's the Story?
Toronto, 1969 24-25

Chuck's Music,
Milwaukee, 1997 26

WTC Shoe Shine Man,
New York City, August, 2001 29

*Sweet Dreams in Great
Grandmother's Bassinet,*
Manhattan, 2001 30

Rugby, Milwaukee, 1969 33

Girls from Three Tribes,
Nepal, 1974 34

Crystal Pier,
San Diego, 2000....................36-37

Hat Day,
Manhattan, 2001 38-39

School Children,
Nara, Japan, 2001 40-41

New Year's Eve,
Hotel Del Coronado,
San Diego, 1998 42

Acknowledgments

A special thank you to our colleagues and friends who reviewed this manuscript and offered their encouragement and suggestions: Pat and Roy Mercer, Sue and Bob Rakow, Mike Baldwin, Debra Stefl, David Wells, Kelly Hansen, and Marsh Kadwit.

Also we would like to extend our appreciation to Ron, Carline, and Kathy Zabler, who have printed Todd's photos for more than 34 years, and to Kate Hawley whose creativity was a tremendous asset during the book's initial development process.

In addition, we would like to express our gratitude to Elizabeth Poyet at Peter Pauper Press for her invaluable insights and belief in this publication.

Finally, thank you to all the subjects of these photographs who have been captured on film living their lives in meaningful ways. What they do really does matter and we are pleased to share their joy for life with you.

Susan and Todd Montgomery

About Todd and Susan Montgomery

Todd Montgomery has been photographing the life around him for more than 35 years. Todd's diverse background as naval officer during the Vietnam War, investment manager, and world traveler has allowed him to view humanity from many perspectives. His photos, both silver gelatin and color, cover the range of his experiences all over the U.S., Asia, and Europe. While the themes in his photography are varied, his work focuses on key moments that capture the essence of the subjects. The Agora Gallery in Soho, New York City, exhibited Todd's work at a show in December, 2001.

Susan Montgomery has been writing and producing books throughout her business career. Susan's published writing spans the fields of health care, business, and travel. She has published a variety of books, newsletters, and publications through her communications company, which she has operated for more than two decades.

Susan and Todd, who combined their families 20 years ago, have raised four now-adult children and are involved in the lives of their two grandchildren. They travel around the world studying, photographing, and writing about the cultures they encounter. Susan and Todd divide their time between Wisconsin, New York City, and La Jolla, California.

Do you have a photo that shows what really matters?

Do you have a photo that captures the spirit of what really matters in life? If so, please send a duplicate to the address below for possible inclusion in the next edition of What Really Matters Now. (Sorry——photos cannot be returned.) Please include the name and address of the photographer, and where and when the photo was taken. We will contact you if your photo is selected.

Mail photo to: Chestnut Communications, Inc.
2616 E. Jarvis St.
Shorewood, WI 53211
(414) 967-9952

Or, e-mail photo to: chestnutcom@aol.com